Workbook for Joseph Nguyen's
Don't Believe Everything You Think

Exercises for Reflection, Processing, and Practising the Lessons

 BIG ACTION BOOKS

BigActionBooks.com

Contents

Introduction	3
Chapter 1: The Journey to Find The Root Cause of Suffering	4
Chapter 2: The Root Cause of All Suffering	6
Chapter 3: Why Do We Even Think?	9
Chapter 4: A Guide to Stop Thinking	10
Chapter 5: If we can only feel what we're thinking, don't we need to think positively to feel that way?	12
Chapter 6: How the Human Experience is Created - The Three Principles	14
Chapter 7: How do we stop thinking, if this is the root cause of our suffering?	15
Chapter 8: How can we thrive in a world without thinking?	16
Chapter 9: If we stop thinking, what about our goals, ambitions and dreams?	17
Chapter 10: Unconditional Love & Creation	20
Chapter 11: What do you do next after experiencing joy, love, peace and fulfilment?	22
Chapter 12: Nothing is either good or bad	23
Chapter 13: Without thinking, how do we know what to do?	24
Chapter 14: How to Follow Your Intuition	25
Chapter 15: Creating Space for Miracles	27
Chapter 16: Potential Obstacles When You Live in Non-Thinking	29
Key Takeaways and Practical Exercises	30
Framework for How To Stop Thinking	30
Step-by-step Framework to Curb Overthinking	32
Reflection Prompts	34
Step-by-step Framework for Removing Thinking Triggers	35
1. List your thinking triggers.	35
2. Organize them into categories.	36
3. Rank your list.	36
Step-by-step Framework for Creating a Non-Thinking Environment	38
1. Sort the contents of your list into categories.	38
2. Rank the items in each category.	39
3. Create an action item.	40
4. Create a morning routine.	40
5. Start your day right.	41
6. Begin your day in a peaceful state.	41
Step-by-step Framework for Implementing Non-Thinking Into Your Work	42
1. Compile a list of tasks in your job that deplete your energy.	42
2. Compile a list of tasks in your job that invigorate you.	42
3. Rate each activity on a scale from 1-10.	43
4. Eliminate energy draining activities and do more energy giving activities.	43
5. Work towards the goal.	43
A Guide To Overcoming Destructive Habits & Behaviours	45

Claim your free bonus

There's a free bonus waiting for you as thanks for picking up this workbook. We think you'll like it. Inside, you'll find a list of the most impactful self development books from this year, including:

- Top books for self-growth and mindfulness
- Top books for financial growth
- Top books for relationships (including yourself)
- Top books for productivity and "Getting Things Done"

We hope they provide a little inspiration for you - and perhaps some new discoveries.

To get your free bonus, scan the QR code below or visit BigActionBooks.com/bonus.

Scan to get your free bonus

Introduction

Uncover the root cause of mental suffering - and how to find peace.

WHY THIS WORKBOOK?
You've read Joseph Nguyen's fabulous book about discovering the core of psychological suffering and how to shape a life of peace and joy. Now it's time to actually *practice* it - write; journal; put the lessons in motion.

This workbook was created as a **companion** to Joseph Nguyen's "*Don't Believe Everything You Think: Why Your Thinking Is The Beginning & End Of Suffering*". While reading the book, we found ourselves wishing for a place where we could write, process and practise the book's exercises in a constructive, concise way. The exercises are excellent - but there isn't much space to actually write in the book itself. Instead, we found ourselves cobbling them together in various places - notebooks, journals, pieces of paper - all of which would eventually get lost, or at the very least, not be helpful in putting the lessons into practice. That's how this workbook was born.

HOW TO USE THIS WORKBOOK
This workbook is like a faithful friend to Don't Believe Everything You Think. You'll find all the exercises from the book, summarised and formatted, with space to answer.

- All exercises from Don't Believe Everything You Think, extracted into one single place
- Space to write under each exercise
- Lists, ruled lines and space for you to answer, journal and reflect
- Clearly organised and well-formatted so it's easy to follow

In each section, we've extracted the main premise of the exercise, and then added space to respond and practise the lessons. This may come in the format of a table to fill in, space to free-write, or other exercise methods to provide space for reflection. You'll also notice the "Parts" and "Chapters" referenced in the book, so you can easily find the section if you need to look back on it for further context.

If you want to not only read about how to overcome anxiety, self-doubt, and worry - but also put the lessons into practice - this workbook, as well as your own dedication, will help you do just that.

Enjoy, and thank you.
Let's dive in!

Chapter 1: The Journey to Find The Root Cause of Suffering

In this first chapter, the author sets outs some key tenets for the remainder of the book, notably:

- That when suffering comes our way, we receive two 'arrows' (according to the Buddha):
  → Arrow 1: Physical pain;
  → Arrow 2: Emotional or mental pain.
- It is this second arrow - the emotional and mental pain - where we have a choice in how we react, and whether or not we avoid some or all of this suffering.
- He also notes that it's generally a given that we all would avoid suffering if given the choice (and/or if we knew how).

With this in mind - in which ways have you tried in your own life, to avoid suffering? Are there techniques or methods you have studied which align to the author's comments here? If yes, what are the things you've tried so far, and how did they turn out?

> **Note:** Throughout this workbook, you'll see examples in some places, listed in *grey handwriting like this*. These are just to give you an idea of the kind of action points you might like to take - but feel free to use or ignore them as best suits your style. There's also a section at the back of this notebook for free-form notes and journaling.

Reflections:

Examples:

Studying spiritual texts with a view to curbing suffering

Make a conscious choice to take 5 deep breaths each time I receive some disturbing news

_____

_____

_____

_____

The author also notes here that he, at various times, has tried a lot of different techniques to curb suffering and improve his mindset. These have included:
- Retreats, meditation
- Learning to meditate
- Reading dozens of books
- Changing his diet
- Counselling and learning from mentors
- Researching religions
- And more.

Even still, he vulnerably shares how he didn't feel 'complete' after trying so many techniques, and that at many times he still felt lost and unsure what to do next.

As a precursor for further work we'll do later in this workbook - what have you experimented with so far, in your own journey of self-improvement?

So far I have tried:

_____

_____

_____

_____

_____

_____

Chapter 2: The Root Cause of All Suffering

Recall the examples from the book of how our own 'reality' can be vastly different from other people in the same situation as us:

- Two people sitting in a coffee shop - one experiencing a midlife crisis, the other calmly watching people go by; even though they're in the same place, at the same time, drinking the same drink
- Everybody has a different perception of what money means to them; even though in reality money is the same thing to everybody;
- Everyone has their own opinion of the current president; even though they're all describing the same person.
- The person who hates their job, and even when they're not at work, fumes at the idea of needing to go back to work.

Our own feelings, therefore, come from our own <u>thinking</u> about external events, not from the events themselves. So we can only ever feel what we are thinking.

Nguyen arrived at the conclusion that: *"The root cause of suffering is our own thinking"*.

To practice working on this, think of 3 recent scenarios where your reality has been <u>negatively</u> altered by your own thinking, and ask yourself the question: **Who would I be without this negative thought?** What comes up?

Example:

Negative thinking:
I dislike my job and feel angry when I think about it. Recently while spending time with friends, I zoned out for half of the time because I was consumed by thoughts about the job and how unhappy I am when I'm working.

Who would I be without this negative thought?
Happy, peaceful, free, light. I would have less weight on my shoulders, and be able to be more present and physically enjoy time with friends.

Your turn - think of 3 recent events or thought patterns, and note them down below:

Event #1 - Negative thinking:

_____

_____

_____

_____

Event #1 - Who would I be without this negative thought?

_____

_____

_____

_____

Event #2 - Negative thinking:

_____

_____

_____

_____

Event #2 - Who would I be without this negative thought?

_____

_____

_____

_____

Event #3 - Negative thinking:

_____

_____

_____

_____

Event #3 - Who would I be without this negative thought?

_____

_____

_____

_____

Chapter 3: Why Do We Even Think?

Here we examine why it is that, as humans, we have developed the ability to think and rationalize. In many ways this serves us well, as it allows us to:

- Become aware of danger and react to threatening situations
- Scan our surroundings
- Reference our past experiences to help us make better decisions
- In essence, the job of our mind us to **keep us alive**

Sometimes when we don't understand the mind's mission - to not let us die - it can be difficult to know why we think the way we do. Our consciousness, on the other hand, has a different mission: to help us feel <u>fulfilled</u>. The author suggests that we need to rely (much!) less on our minds - by becoming aware of our thoughts - and instead allow our consciousness and our soul to guide us, as this leads to more fulfilment in an world where we very rarely (if ever) come into true physical danger.

What are some recent situations where you have listened to your mind and let it take the reigns? If this situation were to come up again, how might you be able to react differently?

Situation	How might I react differently next time? (Paying less attention to the mind)
An argument with my partner which turned into a verbal face-off.	Rather than trying to rationalize the situation, listen to the body - note signs of anger and frustration. Take some deep breaths to calm down; return to the argument in 30 minutes.

Chapter 4: A Guide to Stop Thinking

This chapter explores the difference between **thoughts** and **thinking**:

Thoughts *are*:	Thoughts are *not*:
A noun - something we 'have'	A verb - something we 'do'
Something that just 'happens' - no effort	Something we can control - they just come up.

Thinking, on the other hand, is a verb -

Thinking *is*:	Thinking is *not*:
The act of thinking about our thoughts	Something we <u>must</u> engage in (it's optional)
Something which needs energy and effort	
Actively engaging with a thought that has come up in the mind	
The root of our mental suffering	

Which the author summarises as: **Thoughts create. Thinking destroys.**

To illustrate, let's create a space to do the exercise proposed in this chapter:

Step 1: Think about how much money you want to make in a year. Write it down below:

_____

Step 2: Think about that number. In other words, think about that 'thought' of the number itself. How did you feel when you thought about it, how you might achieve it, etc.?

The author suggests that we'll likely feel *positively* about step 1, but be overwhelmed by step 2 when we start 'thinking about the thought'.

The last section of this chapter illustrates a helpful table to help us distinguish whether thoughts and feelings are coming from a **thought** or from the **thinking mind**. Use this as a reference point, and note down any reflections below:

Attribute	Thought	Thinking Mind
Source	Universe	Ego
Weight	Light	Heavy
Energy	Expansive	Restrictive/confined
Nature	Infinite	Limiting
Quality	Creative	Destructive
Charge	Positive	Negative
Essence	Divine/Everlasting	Mortal
Feeling	Alive	Stressful
Emotion	Love	Fear
Belief	Infinite Possibilities	Confining
Sense	Wholeness	Separateness
Effort	Effortless	Laborious/difficult

Reflections on the above:

_____

_____

_____

_____

Chapter 5: If we can only feel what we're thinking, don't we need to think positively to feel that way?

This chapter builds on the previous chapters by introducing a more specific nuance: *that we can only feel negative emotions when we're thinking*. Some of these can be helpful, for example in situations where we need to be protected or are in danger.

Recall a time when you felt joy and love on a grand scale. Try to immerse yourself in that situation for at least 30 seconds, really feel into it and be there. What thoughts were going through your head at that time?

_____

_____

_____

_____

_____

The author asserts that most likely, you:
- Didn't have any thoughts going through your mind at that time. You simply felt the joy, love, happiness, gratitude, etc.
- If you <u>did</u> have those thoughts at the time - they were probably <u>already there</u> before you started thinking them.

Why? Because <u>being</u> joy, love, freedom, gratitude and ecstasy is our <u>natural</u> way of being.

Next, think of a time when you felt extremely stressed or anxious. How much thinking was going on at the time? What were you thinking about?

_____

_____

_____

The author mentions a great lesson he received from a mentor:
- Imagining the mind as a speedometer, similar to that of a car
- And thoughts-per-minute instead of miles-per-hour
- **The more thoughts, the higher the thought-o-meter goes**; and when we get into the red zone, we can start to feel stressed, anxious, burned out, and frustrated.
- Lastly, that it's not <u>what</u> we are thinking, but <u>that we are thinking</u>, which causes suffering.

Thought-o-meter

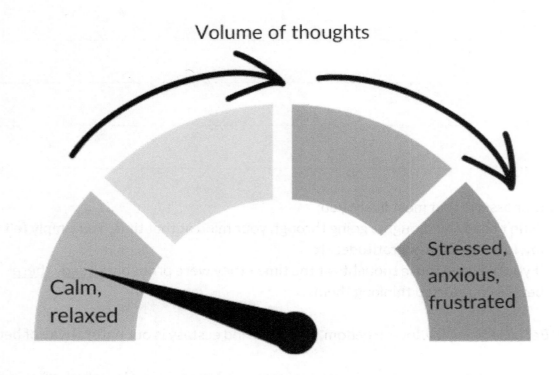

Volume of thoughts

Calm, relaxed

Stressed, anxious, frustrated

Chapter 6: How the Human Experience is Created - The Three Principles

This chapter discusses the human experience at a fundamental level being driven by three core principles:

1. Universal Mind: The intelligence behind all living beings. Energy and life force that exists in everything - an acorn's ability to grow into a tree, plants staying in orbit, and our bodies' ability to heal.
2. Universal Consciousness: The <u>collective</u>, unified consciousness of all things. This creates our awareness of our own existence and the ability to perceive our own thoughts. This is basic 'awareness'.
3. Universal Thought: Our ability to think and create form from the Universal Mind's energy. The 'thing' or the 'object' we are able to perceive through consciousness (#2 above). Without it, we would have nothing to be aware of.

In which ways can you relate to the 3 principles above? What are your reflections upon reading about them phrased in this way?

_____

_____

_____

_____

_____

_____

_____

_____

_____

Chapter 7: How do we stop thinking, if this is the root cause of our suffering?

Whilst it's not possible to stop thinking all together, with practice and work we can gradually reduce the amount of thinking we do over time, and move towards a state of 'being' and live in a more blissful state for more time than we do now.

We're not trying to stop thoughts in general - we want to allow thoughts to flow, but reduce our attachment and thinking <u>about</u> those thoughts.

The way to do it? Awareness. As the author says *"The most paradoxical thing is that we don't need to do anything to stop thinking other than: **be aware of it**"*.

Recall the analogy from the book: If we had a bowl of dirty water and were asked to clean it, we may be tempted to boil it, filter it, etc. Whereas if we just **let it sit**, gradually it will settle and become clear.

→ If your mind starts to feel 'cloudy' or 'dirty', the way to clear it up is to simply be aware of it and let it settle. This is a way to recognize an indicator of too much thinking.

Try practicing this for the next 3 days, and observe what happens. Note your reflections below, recording the situation, what you did, and the outcome:

_____

_____

_____

_____

_____

_____

_____

_____

Chapter 8: How can we thrive in a world without thinking?

Think of a recent time when you were in a 'flow' state and doing your best work, totally captivated by the moment - what **thoughts are going through your head**?

_____

_____

_____

_____

_____

As the author notes, most likely, the answer that comes up is: I wasn't having any thoughts at all. We mostly do our best work when we're in a state of 'flow' and we're not thinking at all. We're so engrossed in the moment that we don't need to think; rather, we're in a <u>natural</u> state of peak performance.

In the case of professional athletes and olympians, the author argues that thinking actually *hinders* their performance - when we hesitate, are insecure or are acting fearful, we are not at our best.

It's in this way that we can not only 'operate' in a thinking-free state, but actually flourish in it.

Reflections:

_____

_____

_____

_____

Chapter 9: If we stop thinking, what about our goals, ambitions and dreams?

This chapter delves into several key themes, which we shall break down here.

I think, therefore I suffer
Here we examine several key questions, such as:

- If we stop thinking (in order to end or curtail suffering as mentioned earlier), how do we actually live our lives?
- What happens with dreams, wants and ambitions?
- Do we all just need to stop what we're doing, and either watch TV mindlessly or become monks and live in the mountains?

Of course, that is not the answer. Rather, what the author suggests is recognizing the difference between **thoughts** and **thinking**.

What was your initial impression upon reading this? Did you understand the distinction and see it as a way of curbing suffering?

_____

_____

_____

_____

_____

Goals come from one of two sources: Either <u>in</u>spiration or <u>des</u>peration.
Desperation-created goals tend to come from a place of scarcity, not having 'enough', and a rush to do things. This can feel like a heavy load and a daunting path to take, and is usually directed towards an extrinsic or external goal, outside of ourselves.

Inspiration-created goals, on the other hand, feel like a 'calling', they feel inspiring and expansive, almost limitless, and like they are just waiting to emerge from us. These kinds of goals tend to be much more intrinsically-driven - we want to do it because we want to do it, not as a means to a different end.

How do we know if a dream is created from a base of inspiration or desperation?
Energetically, inspiration-driven goals have an energetic feeling of abundance, ease, flow, joy, and don't feel like 'work' or a 'burden'. Desperation-driven goals on the other hand feel like an obligation, something we 'have' to do, restrictive, limited and heavy.

When we follow 'inspiration' rather than 'desperation', the key is to avoid getting swept up in the <u>thinking</u> about that inspiration or idea. When we begin to think about the thought - as mentioned earlier - we fall back into analyzing and being limited by our thoughts, and more easily fall into negativity. Rather, when feeling an inspiration-driven goal, when we follow that for what it is, we feel fulfilment, peace and joy.

What goals in your life have come (or are currently coming) from a place of inspiration VS desperation?

Inspiration-driven Goals	Desperation-driven Goals
Examples: *Feeling the urge to create a new business based on a passion of yours* *Writing music, painting, or writing poetry*	*Examples:* *Wanting to leave a bad relationship* *Wanting to leave a job you don't like*

Of the list you created above, what are the **top 2-3 goals** you'd like to pursue further? These might be exactly as you'd noted them above (just a narrowed down list), or some goals reframed with an inspirational base instead of a desperation-driven one.

My top inspiration-driven goals I'd like to pursue further:

_____

_____

_____

_____

Taking it a step further - consider the following question and note down what comes to mind (as <u>thoughts</u> not <u>thinking</u>!): *If you had unlimited money, had already travelled the entire world, were fearless and got no recognition, what would you create?*

_____

_____

_____

_____

_____

_____

_____

Chapter 10: Unconditional Love & Creation

This chapter explores the notion of unconditional love, through the author's relationship with his partner:

- He was able to list dozens of specific reasons why he loved his partner
- Whereas his partner's answer to why she loved him was: *"I don't know, I just do."*
- After a lot of reflection, he realized that her love was unconditional - she loved him as-is. Whereas his need to rationalize a list of 'reasons' why he loved her, gave the impression that if she stopped doing those things (stopped laughing, stopped being generous, etc.) that his love for her would fade -- which of course was not true.

In which areas of your life would you like to cultivate this kind of unconditional love, moving away from 'judgements', 'reasons' and 'rationalizations', and instead leaning into loving 'just because you do'?

_____

_____

_____

_____

_____

_____

Unconditional Creation

When we create, if that creation is driven by an external want - to buy new things, to impress someone, to have a sense of achievement - ultimately that will fade and we're left to pursue a new goal.

In addition to this, all creation goals are inherently linked to the desire to create a <u>feeling</u>:

- Make more money → Feel safe or relaxed
- Spend time with family → Feel love and joy

Goals or objects can't create those feelings for us - it must come from within.

Unconditional creation is creating without a reason or link to another purpose - creating purely for the joy and want to create it. This is creation from a place of abundance. When we create from this baseline, we're much more likely to experience feelings of fulfilment, wholeness and satisfaction. We're only able to pursue unconditional creation with the non-thinking mind - this is what creates 'flow', fulfilment and doing things for the pure joy of it.

In which areas of your life would you like to cultivate unconditional creation - not create with an 'end' or 'goal' in mind (such as money, recognition, etc.), but just for the pure joy of creating?

_____

_____

_____

_____

_____

_____

Chapter 11: What do you do next after experiencing joy, love, peace and fulfilment?

Once you've experienced the peace of non-thinking and being in the present, the author gives us some suggestions as to what to do next:

- You may feel worried, anxious and doubtful because you've just let go of something you'd long-held dear - that thinking prevents suffering, rather than creating it. The realisations outlined in this book can cause damage to the personal ego, which can take time to recognise and adjust to.
- You may also have a lot of additional mental bandwidth due to having reduced your time spent 'thinking'. This bandwidth can instead be directed towards creating goals of inspiration.
- Create an Activation Ritual to get into a state of non-thinking and flow.

What would you like to create or add to your morning routine, to allow space for an Activation Ritual? How can you use this to move towards inspiration-driven goals?

_____

_____

_____

_____

_____

_____

_____

Chapter 12: Nothing is either good or bad

Just as there are no 'wrong' keys on a piano - only notes that sound more or less pleasant when played with other notes - so it is that there are also no 'wrong' decisions in life. There is only <u>thinking that generates more or less pleasant feelings.</u>

Rather than looking for 'good', 'bad', 'right', 'wrong' in the world, we should look for truth instead. When confronted with negative emotions, try to go 'inside' yourself and find the <u>true</u>, deeper reason for it - not external reasons, as this will not give you the answer.

Most negative emotions come from thinking and from misunderstandings. We believe what we're thinking and therefore slip into feeling those negative emotions, generated by negative thinking. The key is to remember the root cause of our suffering: *thinking*.

What are some areas in your life where you've made judgments about something being 'good' or 'bad', that you'd like to let go of?

_____

_____

_____

_____

_____

_____

_____

_____

_____

Chapter 13: Without thinking, how do we know what to do?

When making decisions, the author emphasises relying on non-thinking - and notes that usually we already know what to do, deep down, but we overanalyse which causes us unnecessary suffering. This non-thinking decision-making ability is often called our gut feeling or intuition. Our gut feeling will take us where we need to go, although the path we use to get there is often unknown.

What are some key things you've been considering (or perhaps overanalysing) that you already know, intuitively, what to do but have been delaying in favour of waiting for external approval or validation? *What do you already know you need to do?*

_____

_____

_____

_____

What are some situations from the **past** where you wish you had trusted your 'gut' or your 'intuition'? This is not to judge ourselves but rather to bring to the surface the fact that we have most likely already had situations where we knew what to do.

_____

_____

_____

_____

Chapter 14: How to Follow Your Intuition

In this chapter, we learn that being in a state of "flow", or as the author calls it, "non-thinking", isn't restricted to only certain activities, such as those we love to do. Rather, he asserts that we can be in a state of non-thinking any time we choose - as long as this is in the present moment.

It's for this reason that wider teachings such as masters and mentors, often talk about the importance of being in the present moment - the only time we can be in 'flow'.

In addition, when we follow our intuition or 'gut feel', rather than our thinking mind, we are trusting ourselves and the fact that we already have the built-in knowledge of what we need to do, without resorting to over-thinking.

What does following our intuition look like?
- We're tapped into something greater than ourselves
- State of flow - often losing track of time and not thinking constantly about next steps
- Lose our sense of 'self' (in a good way) and become one with where we are at the present moment
- You have a gut feeling that you 'should' do something, but can't explain why

This often leads to larger impacts, such as business success, chance meetings, money coming in at the right time, and so-on.

How do you feel about this? Have you had any instances when this has happened to you?

_____

_____

_____

_____

_____

_____

_____

Usually, after experiencing this - being in a state of flow and 'letting go' of the thinking mind, which is sometimes followed by things 'falling into place' without us forcing it - we tend to **revert back to** thinking and proactively 'figuring things out'. This is when we begin to lose our power - instead, it's better to recognize that we can't possibly 'figure out' all the complexities of this world, and instead trust our instincts instead of our thinking mind.

Have you had times where something great has happened while following your intuition, and then you've lapsed back into 'thinking' again? What could you do to avoid this?

Reflections:

_____

_____

_____

_____

_____

_____

_____

_____

_____

_____

_____

_____

_____

Chapter 15: Creating Space for Miracles

In this chapter we begin with the story of the student and the Zen monk. The student is so full of his own ideas and stories, that he isn't able to listen to any advice from the master. To illustrate this, the master overfills the student's cup as a metaphor, then requests for him to come back with an empty cup.

This is a powerful metaphor for when we need to 'empty our cup', or create space for new ideas and actions to flow into us.

In what ways do you sometimes (or often) over-fill your cup? Do you regularly make empty space for 'nothing', so that there is room for other things to flow in, based on your intuition?

_____

_____

_____

_____

_____

We also encounter the story of Thomas Edison, who would nap in his chair holding steel balls. Eventually he would fall into a state of deep sleep - the steel balls would drop to the floor - and often he would wake up with a solution to the problem he'd been wanting to solve.

How could you create your own 'steel cup' exercise? What brings you back to non-thinking? This could be things like a nap, meditation, exercise, nature, playing music, and so-on. What are some 'steel cup' exercises you can implement for yourself?

_____

_____

_____

Meditation from the book for receiving 'downloads' and creating space for the mind to solve problems on its own:

1. Be aware that thinking is the root cause of all our negative emotions. Reflect on this.
2. Give up on any manual thinking, to create space. Have faith that your inner wisdom, gut feeling and intuition will give you the answer. Surrender to the fact that this may take time, and may not come in the form you would expect. Let go of expectations.
3. Monitor any feelings that arise as you give up control. Magnify positive feelings such as love, joy and peace. Whatever is coming your way, aim to meet it with love, and the answer will come to you.

Reflections

_____

_____

_____

_____

_____

_____

_____

_____

_____

_____

Chapter 16: Potential Obstacles When You Live in Non-Thinking

As we delve further into the non-thinking approach, the author forewarns us that we're likely to hit some obstacles along the way. And that's okay! Be aware of the following:

- A reduction in stress. Many worries may simply disappear as you don't see them as problems any more. You may feel strong feelings of peace and serenity with this.
- Uncertainty. As humans, we fear uncertainty by nature - it's natural to feel at odds and unsure about this new feeling of peace. Have faith that things will work out well, trust your intuition, and know that the world is working *with you*, not against you.
- You might fall back into thinking again. That's okay, as it's a process. Try not to be judgemental about it or beat yourself up. Simply start again once you catch yourself.

Notes and reflections:

_____

_____

_____

_____

_____

_____

_____

_____

_____

Key Takeaways and Practical Exercises

The following sections provide notes, space and exercises for the 'practical takeaways' section at the back of the original book. Feel free to complete some or all of them. You might like to do everything - or, you might like to pick and choose which area is most challenging for you currently - for example, work-related thinking - and start there.

Framework for How To Stop Thinking

- Remove elements that may heighten your inclination for overthinking (or situations that trigger your fight or flight response).

  What kinds of triggers often come up for you? What causes you to shift into 'thinking'?

  _____

  _____

  _____

- Minimize uninspiring or unexciting elements and actions in your daily life. What things are you currently finding uninspiring that you might consider removing?

  _____

  _____

  _____

- Create an environment conducive to entering a thought-free state. What could you do to foster this in your day-to-day environment?

  _____

  _____

  _____

- Develop a morning routine for a calm, thought-free start to your day. Use this time to access insights from the boundless wisdom to guide you through life.

   What morning routine would you like to create?

   _____

   _____

   _____

   _____

- Allocate time in your daily schedule for unwinding, relaxation, and returning to a thought-free state. Outline activities you can engage in during your day to accomplish this. Options may include writing in a journal, taking a leisurely stroll, practicing meditation, spending quality time with your pets, enjoying a short nap, partaking in yoga, or any other calming pursuit.

Thing I can do to relax:

Playing with my pets

1. _____

2. _____

3. _____

4. _____

5. _____

6. _____

7. _____

8. _____

9. _____

Step-by-step Framework to Curb Overthinking

1. Recognize that our thoughts are at the core of all suffering (the true nature of thinking).
   - Recognize that if you're experiencing distress, it's a result of your thoughts.
   - Distinguish between the act of thinking and your individual thoughts.
   - Don't seek to pinpoint the source; thinking itself is the primary cause.

Reflections:

_____

_____

_____

_____

_____

_____

_____

2. Create a space for negative thoughts.
   - Allow their presence, and recognize them for what they represent.
   - Acknowledge that you are the space embracing these emotions, yet you are not the emotions themselves.
   - Don't shy away from solitary contemplation and have the bravery to let it into your awareness.
   - Embrace it and understand that these thoughts merely seek acknowledgment.
   - Recognize that pessimistic thoughts only wield influence if you invest in them.
   - Once you grant them space within your consciousness without resistance, you can then delve beyond the emotions to uncover the underlying reality.
   - Each emotion carries a kernel of truth within, enabling you to enhance your awareness and embrace a richer experience of life.

Note your reflections on the next page →

Reflections:

_____

_____

_____

_____

_____

_____

_____

_____

3. After recognizing your thoughts, let them flow without holding onto them. This will naturally lead to positive emotions such as serenity, affection, and happiness. Embrace these emotions when they emerge. If the negative sensation lingers, return to step 1 and continue until you've discovered some peace.

Reflection:

_____

_____

_____

_____

_____

_____

Reflection Prompts

On a scale of 1-10, how much did you think today? (1 being low, 10 being high)

1	2	3	4	5	6	7	8	9	10

What percentage of your day was spent in fight or flight mode?

Fight/flight mode:

0%	10%	20%	30%	40%	50%	60%	70%	80%	90%	100%

What percentage was spent in a relaxed, calm state?

0%	10%	20%	30%	40%	50%	60%	70%	80%	90%	100%

Notes/insights from the above:

_____

_____

_____

_____

_____

_____

_____

_____

Step-by-step Framework for Removing Thinking Triggers

1. List your thinking triggers.

Conduct a review to identify factors that might increase your vulnerability to thoughts, and create a list.

A. Jot down all your thoughts. It can be beneficial to tap into your instincts and gauge the impact of your environment on your well-being. If you're in a tranquil and composed state, the answer will become clear.

B. If you're struggling to generate ideas, try to recall situations that trigger your fight-or-flight response, induce anxiety, or lead to excessive thinking. Anything that thrusts you into survival mode will hinder your ability to remain thought-free.

C. If you're still finding it challenging to identify these situations, consider keeping a journal throughout the week and document anything that triggers your fight-or-flight response. You'll have a useful list by the week's end.

My thinking triggers:

1. _____

2. _____

3. _____

4. _____

5. _____

6. _____

7. _____

8. _____

9. _____

10. _____

2. Organize them into categories.

Sort the items you've jotted down into different categories.

A. Here are a few examples of categories:

I. Physical Health

a. What substances, when consumed, can heighten the likelihood of triggering a fight or flight reaction, leading to anxiety, stress, or prolonged overthinking? This includes food, stimulants, beverages, and so on.

II. Physical Environment

b. Which elements in your immediate surroundings can increase the likelihood of triggering a fight or flight reaction, leading to anxiety, stress, or prolonged overthinking?

III. Digital Environment

c. Which items on your phone, computer, or TV can increase your likelihood of triggering a fight or flight reaction (anxiety, stress, prolonged overthinking)?

IV. Digital Consumption

d. Which types of media or content you expose yourself to can heighten the likelihood of triggering a fight or flight reaction (anxiety, stress, prolonged overthinking)?

3. Rank your list.

Once you've sorted everything into categories, rearrange your list and start prioritizing the items based on their impact on you, starting with the most significant.

Thinking Triggers	Category	Rank

Thinking Triggers	Category	Rank

4. Create an action item.

Select the most important items from each list and devise a plan for addressing them to reduce their presence in your surroundings. Focus on tasks that are feasible and won't add to your stress levels; this way, you'll achieve the exercise's intended benefits. Begin with minor changes, and once you're comfortable with the adjustments and their positive effects, you can consider eliminating other factors.

Thinking Triggers	Category	Rank	Action Plan

Notes/insights from the above:

_____

_____

_____

_____

_____

_____

Step-by-step Framework for Creating a Non-Thinking Environment

Similar to how we listed out potential triggers in the previous exercise, next, we're going to apply this to creating an environment for positivity and relaxation. Make a list of all the factors that enable you to get into a calm, tranquil, thought-free state. These could be activities such as physical fitness, mindfulness, listening to specific music genres, your surroundings, and so forth.

Things that relax me:

1. _____

2. _____

3. _____

4. _____

5. _____

6. _____

7. _____

8. _____

9. _____

10. _____

1. Sort the contents of your list into categories.

Examples Of Categories:

I. Physical Health
a. Which substances you consume contribute to your well-being, provide lasting vitality, and promote a sense of tranquillity?

II. Physical Environment
a. Which elements in your surroundings contribute to your connection with your inner self?

III. Digital Environment
a. Which features on your phone, computer, or TV assist you in connecting with your inner self?

IV. Digital Consumption
a. Which types of media/content you engage with contribute to a sense of alignment with your inner self?

2. Rank the items in each category.

Prioritize the items in each category based on their effectiveness in facilitating a state of non-thinking, starting with the most influential and ending with the least influential.

Things That Relax Me	Category	Rank

3. Create an action item.

Select the most important elements from each list and devise a plan for integrating them into your daily routine. Avoid taking on too many changes at once, as it can become daunting. Start with what you can comfortably handle for now, and gradually introduce more once you've adapted to your new routine.

Things That Relax Me	Category	Rank	Action Plan

4. Create a morning routine.

Establish an empowering daily practice or morning regimen that facilitates your transition into a thought-free state and enables you to connect with your best self. Strategize your preferred morning routine that's feasible at this moment. Begin with modest steps and steer clear of overburdening yourself. Make sure to allocate time for personal reflection, such as meditation, yoga, or analogous spiritual exercises that aid you in attuning to Infinite Intelligence.

My morning routine:

- _____

- _____

- _____

- _____

- _____

- _____

- _____

5. Start your day right.

The way you start your day sets the tone for the day ahead. If you kickstart your morning by immediately delving into your phone, emails, and your to-do list, you're essentially beginning your day in a stressful, fight-or-flight mindset that's likely to persist throughout the day.

6. Begin your day in a peaceful state.

When you start your day in a calm state and engage in a daily practice that helps you achieve a thought-free mindset, you'll maintain that flow throughout the day, making it more challenging to become entangled in external distractions that might lead to overthinking and stress. That's why many revered spiritual leaders incorporate morning customs or practices into their routines.

Notes/insights from the above:

_____

_____

_____

_____

_____

_____

_____

Step-by-step Framework for Implementing Non-Thinking Into Your Work

1. Compile a list of tasks in your job that deplete your energy.
Tasks that you find unappealing or burdensome in your job.

1. _____

2. _____

3. _____

4. _____

5. _____

6. _____

7. _____

2. Compile a list of tasks in your job that invigorate you.
What brings about inspiration, vitality, a sense of liveliness, and a feeling of weightlessness.

1. _____

2. _____

3. _____

4. _____

5. _____

6. _____

7. _____

3. Rate each activity on a scale from 1-10.

Review your entire list and assign a score to each activity, ranking them from 1 to 10. Use 1 for activities that sap your energy, and 10 for those that ignite your inspiration and vitality when you engage in them.

Activities	Rating

4. Eliminate energy draining activities and do more energy giving activities.

Weekly, remove 1-3 items from your energy-sapping roster and prioritize engaging in activities rated 9 or 10 on your list.

5. Work towards the goal.

The aim is to reach a stage where 80% of your work hours are devoted to tasks ranking at 9 or 10 on your priority list.

Notes/insights from the above:

A Guide To Overcoming Destructive Habits & Behaviours

As you make room in your life and reduce overthinking, you'll soon notice various unfavourable, harmful patterns you might have that contribute to your vulnerability to suffering. This is perfectly fine. Avoid self-criticism as it can exacerbate the situation. Below, you'll find a more comprehensive guide to assist you in overcoming such detrimental habits.

1. Recognize the specific behaviour you wish to alter and ensure that it's a sincere need for change. Realize that in order to break free from the ongoing cycle of distress, you must be willing to release the beliefs that contribute to that suffering. If you're not committed to this change, there's no reason to proceed, but if you are, let's embark on the journey of relinquishing these beliefs.

Behaviours I want to change:

1. _____

2. _____

3. _____

4. _____

5. _____

6. _____

7. _____

8. _____

9. _____

10. _____

2. Record in precise and thorough detail the occurrences of this behaviour (frequency, timing, etc.). Try to capture this in as much detail as possible.

Note your reflection on the next page →

Behaviours I Want to Change	Details About This Behaviour

3. What's going through your mind just before you start the action? Identify the emotion that sets off the behaviour. Be truthful with yourself.

_____

_____

_____

_____

_____

_____

_____

4. Identify the particular thought processes at play. Elaborate on **what you tell yourself in that moment** with precision.

_____

_____

_____

_____

_____

_____

_____

5. What thoughts or ideas are associated with this habit? What judgments have you formed that make you feel **OBLIGATED** to engage in this action?

_____

_____

_____

_____

_____

_____

_____

6. What are your emotions when you hold that thought?

_____

_____

_____

_____

_____

_____

_____

7. What do you anticipate will occur if you fail to carry out the behaviour? In simpler terms, what do you think will be the results if you don't take the action?

_____

_____

_____

_____

_____

8. Is it a 100% surety that it will happen, if you don't engage in the action?

_____

_____

_____

_____

9. Do you realize the harm in this mindset and how it leads to your distress?

_____

_____

_____

_____

10. Are you ready to release these thoughts and actions at this point?

_____

_____

_____

_____

_____

11. Tap into your inner insight and your best self. What messages does it convey to you? What lessons is it guiding you towards? In what ways does it suggest you bring balance back into your life? How is it encouraging your personal growth at this moment? Allow room for an epiphany from Infinite Intelligence regarding the true reasons behind your need for change.

_____

_____

_____

_____

_____

_____

_____

12. When you get the insight, let yourself really feel the freedom, peace, and joy. Sense that weight lifting off your shoulders. You'll know you've done it right when you physically and energetically feel lighter, and the way you see the action or habit changes. Dive into that deep sense of gratitude and just let yourself be.

13. Record any realizations you've gained and document your recent experiences to create a record of these extraordinary moments in your life.

_____

_____

_____

_____

_____

_____

_____

_____

_____

_____

_____

_____

_____

_____

You made it!
You've completed the workbook.

Claim your free bonus

There's a free bonus waiting for you as thanks for picking up this workbook. We think you'll like it. Inside, you'll find a list of the most impactful self development books from this year, including:

- Top books for self-growth and mindfulness
- Top books for financial growth
- Top books for relationships (including yourself)
- Top books for productivity and "Getting Things Done"

We hope they provide a little inspiration for you - and perhaps some new discoveries.

To get your free bonus, scan the QR code below or visit BigActionBooks.com/bonus.

Scan to get your free bonus

Would you help us with a review?

If you enjoyed the workbook, we'd be so grateful you could help us out by leaving a review on Amazon (even a super short one!). Reviews help us so much - in spreading the word, in helping others decide if the workbook is right for them, and as feedback for our team.

If you'd like to give us any suggestions, need help with something, or to find more workbooks for other self-development books, please visit us at BigActionBooks.com.

Thank you

Thank you so much for picking up the Workbook for Tori Dunlap's *Financial Feminist*. We really hope you enjoyed it, and that it helped you practise the lessons in everyday life.

Thanks again,
The Big Action Books team

 **BIG ACTION BOOKS**

Notes

_____

_____

_____

_____

_____

_____

_____

_____

_____

_____

_____

_____

_____

_____

_____

_____

_____

Notes

_____

_____

_____

_____

_____

_____

_____

_____

_____

_____

_____

_____

_____

_____

_____

Notes

_____

_____

_____

_____

_____

_____

_____

_____

_____

_____

_____

_____

_____

_____

Notes

Notes

_____

_____

_____

_____

_____

_____

_____

_____

_____

_____

_____

_____

_____

Notes

_____

_____

_____

_____

_____

_____

_____

_____

_____

_____

_____

_____

_____

_____

_____

Notes

_____

_____

_____

_____

_____

_____

_____

_____

_____

_____

_____

_____

_____

_____

Made in the USA
Las Vegas, NV
13 December 2024

14088535R00037